MAMA V

Sedona - A Quick & Easy Guide

Copyright © 2022 by Mama V

All rights reserved. No part of this publication may be reproduced, stored or transmitted in any form or by any means, electronic, mechanical, photocopying, recording, scanning, or otherwise without written permission from the publisher. It is illegal to copy this book, post it to a website, or distribute it by any other means without permission.

Mama V asserts the moral right to be identified as the author of this work.

Mama V has no responsibility for the persistence or accuracy of URLs for external or third-party Internet Websites referred to in this publication and does not guarantee that any content on such Websites is, or will remain, accurate or appropriate.

Designations used by companies to distinguish their products are often claimed as trademarks. All brand names and product names used in this book and on its cover are trade names, service marks, trademarks and registered trademarks of their respective owners. The publishers and the book are not associated with any product or vendor mentioned in this book. None of the companies referenced within the book have endorsed the book.

First edition

This book was professionally typeset on Reedsy.
Find out more at reedsy.com

Contents

1	A Brief Introduction	1
2	Getting the Lay of the Land	3
3	Some Fun Things to do in Sedona	5
4	Before You Hit the Trails	11
5	Favorite Hikes	17
6	Red Rock State Park	24
7	Vortex	27
8	Conclusion	32
9	Resources	33

1

A Brief Introduction

Sedona is such a magical place. I remember the first time I ever saw Sedona. I drove from Flagstaff down Oak Creek Canyon. I was in awe! I had never experienced such natural beauty. I made my husband pull over multiple times so I could just bask in the wonder I am still moved by the beauty.

I am writing this to serve as a quick and easy guide to Sedona. There is so much information out there it can be daunting. If you are like me you could spend days researching a travel destination online trying to find the best of the best. My goal is to eliminate the need for you to spend your time engaging in research so you can spend your time enjoying all that Sedona has to offer. This is by no means an exhaustive guide but it will point you in the right direction to make the most of your vacation. This is the same information I share with friends and family.

A little about me, I moved to Sedona in 2012 and poured love and money into restoring a 1980s home. At that time my husband and I had spent more than two years touring homes in Sedona. Our real estate agent must have been a saint! We had pretty much lost hope we would ever be able to find a home that fit our needs at a price we could afford. But then "our" home came on the market. My husband immediately saw its potential, all I saw was lots of choppy rooms and pink carpet. Yes the location was ideal but whoa that 80s vibe was a bit much. Fortunately he prevailed and we purchased the home. We then embarked on a major remodel project, removing walls, raising the roof, updating the kitchen and baths and getting rid of that hideous pink carpet. The end result was a warm, welcoming home, well suited for entertaining. It was such a joy gathering my growing family for holidays. There were two Christmases in a row where pregnancies were announced. Special times for sure. It is my love for Sedona that I share with you and provide you the opportunity to get the most out of your time in this amazing city.

May you find joy and peace during your stay in Sedona!

Mama V

2

Getting the Lay of the Land

Now for some basic information about our city. There are basically three main areas that make up Sedona: Uptown Sedona along 89A as you head towards Oak Creek Canyon (& Flagstaff); West Sedona along 89A as you head towards Cottonwood; and The Village of Oak Creek along 179 as you head towards I-17. It can be confusing because there is an area called The Village of Oak Creek which is many miles away from Oak Creek Canyon. To confuse our dear visitors more, locals will often refer to the roundabout at the interchange of 89A and 179 as the "Y". This is because it was a Y intersection before we went all European with our many roundabouts.

The uptown area is where you can shop to your heart's content and enjoy a variety of dining opportunities. Uptown provides a vast array of goods and services, you could easily spend a whole day here and still not take everything in. If you fancy a Jeep Tour you can connect with a number of vendors while shopping. However, this is not the only premium shopping opportunity Sedona has to offer. A little south of Uptown on 179 is Tlaquepaque, a beautiful place to shop and dine. Across the street from there is Hillside shopping center, with dining and some really cool clothing stores. Staying in Uptown will provide you walking opportunities for shopping and dining. Most people consider Uptown the place with high energy because of its hustle and bustle even though most establishments close early.

West Sedona provides grocery stores, a movie theater, more shopping and the kind of businesses the locals need to make a good life in Sedona. There are a number of lodging options including hotels and vacation rentals scattered around West Sedona, staying in this area will allow for easy access to grocery and restaurants.

Taking the majestic 7.5 mile scenic byway along 179 towards I-17 will lead you to The Village of Oak Creek, also considered Sedona. It has grown up over the past few years and provides a variety of casual dining, easy going coffee shops and an array of lodging options. Most folks consider this community to have a more laid back vibe. It provides ready access to golfing, hikes and great mountain bike trails.

3

Some Fun Things to do in Sedona

Oh the magnificent opportunities for indulgence.

Enjoying Northern Arizona's Burgeoning Wine Industry
   There are many companies that will allow you to taste the wine and even swallow without worrying about driving. Arizona winery tours has a stellar reputation and includes lunch in their package https://www.arizonawinerytours.com/northern-tours. Bliss Wine tours also enjoy rave reviews from their guests https://blissarizona.com/sedona-to-verde-valley.

If you have a designated driver among your group you might consider forgoing the formal tour and create your own Northern Arizona Wine Tour. Check out these three wineries on Page Springs Road in Cornville: **Page Spring Cellars** 1500 N Page Spring Road, **Oak Creek Vineyards and Winery** 1555 N Page Spring Road, **Javelina Leap Vineyard Winery & Bistro** 1565 North Page Springs Road. While in the area you may want to dine at **Up the Creek Bistro and Wine Bar** 1975 N Page Spring Road.

Alternatively consider a drive to Old Town Cottonwood where you can enjoy wine tasting at several different establishments all within a few blocks walk. Old Town Cottonwood boasts a collection of unique shops and some truly great food. I love seeing the transformation that has taken place in Old Town Cottonwood. I enjoy meeting up with friends for a glass of wine at dinner. There are so many good dining options and they are all consolidated within a few blocks. Check it out, you will be glad you did.

Spas

If you are looking for a day of pampering you have so many options. I have listed a few to cut down your search time. Sedona is home to Mii amo https://www.miiamo.com a world class spa located at the Enchantment Resort. Amara Resort and Spa in Uptown Sedona is sure to please with their salt water infinity pool and red rock views https://www.amararesort.com/spa. Los Abrigados Resort and Spa is located behind Tlaquepaque https://www.sedonaspa.com. Many of my house guests have enjoyed their time at Sedona New Day Spa https://www.sedonanewdayspa.com A Spa for You Sedona Day Spa voted travelers choice in 2021 by trip advisor https://www.aspaforyou.com/aspaforyou.htm. For something unconventional try True Rest Float Spa, I have never experienced this one but a dear friend told me it was awesome, https://truerest.com.

Soft Landing

Ballooning

Could there be a more magnificent way to see the Red Rocks? Many years ago before we even moved to Sedona my husband treated me and our two daughters to a balloon ride in Sedona as my Birthday present. It was freaking awesome! Only challenging part was you have to get up really early and it can be really cold up there depending upon the time of year you visit. I have a friend who used to be in the industry and she recommends Red Rock Balloons https://redrockballoons.com/ or Northern Light Balloon Expeditions https://www.northernlightballoon

s.com.

Biking

I know there are some fabulous mountain bike trails but this is not my sport. So I will just send you to the experts at Absolute Bikes https://absolutebikes.net located in The Village of Oak Creek. They have rentals for mountain bikes and road bikes, my son-in-law rode in some races representing them. I can tell you I love their lattes and the staff are really helpful.

In West Sedona you can go to https://thundermountainbikes.com.

Golfing

I am not a golfer so I can't say which of these courses will provide the most challenge, but I can say with great confidence any one of these courses will provide lovely scenery while you play.

Sedona Golf Resort in my opinion is the most beautiful course of these three. It is located in The Village of Oak Creek. It has the added benefit of a nice restaurant. https://www.sedonagolfresort.com

Oakcreek Country Club is an older course also located in The Village of Oak Creek https://www.oakcreekcc.com

Canyon Mesa in a short 9 hole course also located in The Village of Oak Creek https://www.canyonmesacountryclub.com.

Seven Canyons is a **private** golf course, you can take a look at the course here https://sevencanyons.com/golf. If you are enticed and want to play this gorgeous course there is a way, but it will be pricey. You can book a stay at Seven Canyons through this site https://sedona.org/vacation-rentals/seven-canyons/?location_area_id=15118 or stay at the

Enchantment Resort https://www.enchantmentresort.com. A stay at one of these elegant locals will grant you access to this private course but you will still have to pay the golf fees.

Places I Enjoy Eating

My Daughter Outside Mariposa

Mariposa https://www.mariposasedona.com Truly one of the best restaurants for the Red Rock Vistas. I love the menu but some think it a bit pricey. If you are vacationing on a tight budget skip the meal and do appetizers and drinks on the patio at sunset. Located in West Sedona.

Colt Grill https://coltgrill.com/locations Yum yum yum love their smoke brisket. You can find them in The Village of Oak Creek and Old Town Cottonwood.

Cusina Rustica https://www.cucinarustica.com They have a nice wine selection and the best lasagna, my mouth is watering just thinking about it. Located in The Village of Oak Creek

Creekside American Bistro https://creeksidesedona.com Love breakfast at this restaurant. Located near the intersection of 89A and 179.

Oak Creek Brewery and Grill https://oakcreekbreweryandgrill.com Can't beat them for a burger and brew. Located at Tlaquepaque.

4

Before You Hit the Trails

Cell Service: You will likely find many areas where your cell phone does not have reception. This varies by provider and by phone. I have Verizon which generally is the best provider for the greater Sedona area, so I can get service in most places with my phone. However, I can be standing next to someone else with Verizon and they find they have no reception. Go figure so... please know that you could find yourself in a spot where you can not pick up cell service. This means if you are planning on using your phone for online map service it may not work, especially when hiking canyons. This may also impact coordinating with fellow travelers from time to time.

Weather:

People travel from around the world to vacation in Sedona. The weather here is spectacular year round, with average rainfall of 18.94" per year with much of it falling during monsoon season. Monsoon season is my absolute favorite time of year, which generally runs from July to Mid August. Some years are a little longer or shorter and some years they never show up. If you are not familiar with monsoons, here is a little insight on what to expect. In the morning you may notice the sky seems a little hazy and somewhat less vibrant blue. Then you will find thunder heads (those fluffy white clouds) billowing up over the horizon come late afternoon. Then you will hear thunder and see lighting in the distance, get ready because you are likely in for a downpour. You need to plan to be out of harm's way. Monsoons can bring flash floods resulting in water raging through ravines sweeping away everything in its path - make sure that is not you. Also there is risk from lighting strikes if you are out in the open or in elevated areas.

- **Average Temperature Ranges:**
- **January through March** you can expect highs of mid 50s to mid 60 with lows in the 30s
- **April through May** you can expect highs of mid 70s to low 80 with lows in the 40s
- **June through August** you can expect Highs in the 90s to low 100s with lows in the 60s
- **September through October** you can expect Highs of high 80s to high 70s with lows in the 50s
- **November through December** you can expect Highs of high 50s to high 60s with lows in the 30s

This gorgeous masterpiece of nature is located at 4500 feet elevation and on average is basked in 278 days of sunshine per year. Please be sure to carry enough water with you to stay well hydrated, more on this later. Additionally, always wear sunscreen, sun glasses and even a hat would be advisable. If enjoying Sedona in the summer months please remember the summer sun can really take it out of you, so best to plan summer hikes early morning or late afternoon. Even in the winter you need to remember to take precautions as the sun is still shining bright on most days. I enjoy mid day hikes best in the winter months. There is nothing quite as beautiful as a bit of snow resting upon the tops of the red rocks. This doesn't happen very often, but if you have the chance to be here when it snows don't pass up the opportunity. Oh and one word of caution, we desert rats don't know how to drive in the snow, so beware.

Safety Tips

My Daughter and Granddaughter Taking a Break to Power Up

Most Important Hydrate!!

General rule of thumb, on a Sedona summer day you will need to drink a liter of water for every hour you are hiking. In cooler months a ½ liter for every hour may suffice. I have included the average hiking time for each hike. Please bear in mind these times may be vastly underestimated for you, depending upon your fitness level. Be sure that you carry enough water, many people unfamiliar with our desert climate find they need about double the water they consider normal. Have enough water so that you can drink whenever you feel thirsty. Experts recommend you also eat salty snacks like pretzels, potato chips, or nuts. Not only are you losing water you also lose salt which can throw off your electrolytes. Symptoms of dehydration can go unnoticed. For example irritability can be an early sign of dehydration, if your spouse is always grumpy then no they're likely not dehydrated. But keep watching just in case, if they become slow to respond, feel really exhausted, experience muscle weakness or become unable or unwilling to move, dehydration is getting serious. At this point take a rest, find some shade, drink more water, and try pouring some water over your head if you have extra. Left unchecked it can progress to heatstroke which is life threatening. Symptoms of heatstroke include confusion, lack of sweating, headache, flushed (extremely red), rapid heart beat, extreme dry mouth, nausea, vomiting, and delirium. If you or a hiking companion are experiencing signs of heatstroke you need to seek medical attention. Please don't let this be you, take the necessary precautions to keep yourself, your friends, and your family safe.

Things that bite and sting and live in the desert.

We have rattlesnakes but they are generally not very aggressive. If you hear or see a rattlesnake back away and give it a berth of 3 to 4 feet. Scorpions still freak me out but pose little risk when hiking, you are more likely to encounter one indoors. You may find them in the shower or on the floor along exterior walls. Educate inquisitive youngsters so they don't attempt to pick one up. I only know two people who have actually been stung by a scorpion. Out hiking watch when you sit down so that you are not sitting down on something pokey like cati or a scorpion. Indoors you may want to check your shoes before putting them on.

What to wear

Best to wear layers of clothing. A lightweight t-shirt of similar base layer with a cover up suitable for the particular season you are hiking, lighter for summer but more substantial in cooler months. You may think you don't need it but please take note of how the temperature drops in the evenings. Better to have what you need than to be without. Best advice is to always wear high protection sunscreen, sun glasses and a wide brimmed hat. Best for hiking would be a lightweight pair of hiking boots. Many people find a pair of sneakers with good grip work OK. The local hiking club will not let you go out with them if you do not have hiking boots, too many sprained ankles and similar injuries.

My Grandson Making my Heart Skip a Beat

I include these safety tips not to take away from your enjoyment but to enhance it. My kids would tell you I am safety conscious; when we lived in an earthquake prone area, I would frequently point out to them the safest place to take shelter should an earthquake occur.

Just be safe – they don't call me Mama V for no reason. Ha!

5

Favorite Hikes

These hikes are the ones that rise to the top of the list, they are purposely spread across the different areas of Sedona.

General information on parking
   In spring of 2022 Sedona implemented a Shuttle service to aid visitors in getting to many of the more popular trailheads. Because parking at trailheads is limited people would often find they could not hike the trail they desired because the parking lot was already full. For some of the trailheads this could result in overflow parking within the surrounding residential areas creating an unpleasant situation for all concerned. I applaud Sedona leadership for creating a win-win solution. The shuttle service runs year round Thursday through Sunday. It does not service all trailheads, I have identified below if it is a trail served by the shuttle. The shuttle is free. If you are hiking a trail Thursday through Monday with shuttle service you will need this link https://sedonashuttle.com which tells you hours of operation and where to connect with the shuttle and park for free.

Several suggested hikes require a Red Rock Pass (or America The

Beautiful Interagency Pass, Golden Age or Golden Access which you place on the dashboard of your vehicle). No pass is required to just stop and take a picture - read this as less than 15 minutes. Unattended vehicles may be tickets. You can purchase online at https://www.recreation.gov/sitepass/74387 you enter your license plate number for this online option. Passes may also be purchased at most trailheads.

Devil's Bridge Trail (West Sedona)
   Distance: 3.9 Miles Out and Back
   Difficulty: Moderate
   Total Ascent: 521
   Estimated Time: 1 hr 30 min to 2 hrs
   Parking: Monday through Wednesday plan on coming early to secure a parking place.
   A Red Rock Pass (or America The Beautiful Interagency Pass, Golden Age or Golden Access) is required. You can purchase online here https://www.recreation.gov/sitepass/74387
   Thursday through Sunday you will not be able to park here you must use the free shuttle. Click this link to obtain all the latest info https://sedonashuttle.com
   Info: This one is highly popular and with good reason. The first part of this trail is not so special and you need to know there is no shade. The highlight is navigating the beautiful sandstone arch at the end of the trail. The views are beyond description. Don't miss getting your picture on the largest sandstone bridge in the Sedona area.
   Dogs allowed on leash.

West Fork Trail (Beyond Sedona on 89A as you head towards Flagstaff)
   Opens at 8am and closes at dusk
   Distance: 6.5 Miles Out and Back
   Difficulty: Easy to Moderate

Total Ascent: 564 feet

Estimated Time: 2 hr 30min to 4 hrs

Parking: Must pay $11 per car to park (up to 5 people), $2 per person walk in. The parking lot fills up early so you may want to be there at 8 am. If the parking lot is full people park along the road and walk in.

Info: This is one of my very favorite hikes. The trail will meander back and forth over Oak Creek's west fork so you have the opportunity to cool off. You may want to wear water shoes as your feet will get wet. This is a great hike for the kids. Dogs allowed on leash. Toilet available.

Bell Rock Trail

Bell Rock-Courthouse Butte Loop (Village of Oak Creek)
  Distance: 3.9 Mile Loop
  Difficulty: Easy

Total Ascent: 350 feet

Estimated Time: 1hr 30min to 2 hrs 30 min

Parking: Best Choice NorthernMost Bell Rock parking lot

Alternate SouthernMost Bell Rock parking lot which will add 1 mile to hike.

A Red Rock Pass (or America The Beautiful Interagency Pass, Golden Age or Golden Access) is required. You can purchase online here https://www.recreation.gov/sitepass/74387

Info: Bell Rock is one of the most iconic formations in Sedona. It is actually located in what I consider a suburb of Sedona called the Village of Oak Creek. You can go and just hike the Bell Rock area or do the entire loop. My son will sometimes drive down from Flagstaff after work just to do this hike to relax. I like it because it is so conveniently located in the Village of Oak Creek where the vibe is just a little more laid back from the rest of Sedona. Dogs allowed on leash. Toilet available.

Boynton Canyon (Outskirts of West Sedona)

Distance: 6.1 Miles Out and Back

Difficulty: Moderate

Total Ascent: 826 feet

Estimated Time: 2hrs 30min

Parking: Best to arrive early to get a parking space.

A Red Rock Pass (or America The Beautiful Interagency Pass, Golden Age or Golden Access) is required. You can purchase online here https://www.recreation.gov/sitepass/74387

Info: Trail can be hard to follow, most people consider the subway cave to be the best part of this trek. The first part of the trail has a gradual elevation gain, then it kicks it up a notch towards the end. If you get an early start (read this 5ish in the summer) you may enjoy a fair amount of shade along the trail. Please print out a map before you take off and take extra water in case you get lost. I have never heard anyone say they are sorry they made the trek. Dogs allowed on leash. Toilet available. Consider popping onto Enchantment Resort for a bite to eat (probably not a good idea if Fido is in tow). It is gated but don't be intimidated, just let them know you would like to dine with them.

Airport Trail (In town West Sedona)
  Distance: 3 Mile Loop
  Difficulty: Easy to Moderate
  Total Ascent: 415 feet
  Estimated Time: 2 hrs 30min
  Directions: From the junction of Routes 89A and 179, take 89A west 1.0 miles to Airport Road on the left. Go 0.5 miles and park in the turnout on the left.
  Parking: If there is no parking available at the turn out you will need to pay a fee and park at the airport, the red rock pass does not apply to this parking area.
  Info: May not be suitable for children as there are some areas with rather steep drop offs. This hike is easily accessible as it is in the heart of Sedona. It provides a really nice vista of West Sedona. Sunsets can be extra special at this spot as you watch the sun go down and the city lights up as the evening air settles in around you. As always, take plenty of water and put on good footwear as the trail is a little rocky. Dogs allowed on leash.

Cathedral Rock

Cathedral Rock Trail (between Uptown and Village of Oak Creek)
  Distance: 1.2 Miles Out and Back
  Difficulty: Hard
  Total Ascent: 741 feet
  Estimated Time: 1 hr 10 min
  Parking: Monday through Wednesday plan on coming early to secure a parking place.

  A Red Rock Pass (or America The Beautiful Interagency Pass, Golden Age or Golden Access) is required. You can purchase online here https://www.recreation.gov/sitepass/74387

  Thursday through Sunday you will not be able to park here you must use the free shuttle. Click this link to obtain all the latest info https://sedonashuttle.com

  Info: I hesitate adding this one because it is considered a hard climb. If you go to the end of the trail it will require hands and feet to scramble up the last section. You will need to make sure you are wearing hiking boots and physically prepared. However if you just want to soak in the ambiance of Cathedral Rock it will not be that challenging. In the end I decided to include it because it is truly so very special, especially at sunset, and you don't have to go the whole way. So let me know if you braved it and what you thought of the trail. Dogs allowed on leash but not suitable for the last bit which is a climb. Toilet available.

6

Red Rock State Park

Red Rock State Park a Great Place for the Whole Family

Special Mention goes out to Red Rock State Park. This place holds a cherished place in my heart as my youngest daughter exchanged her wedding vows here. It's a great location for a family day of fun. An interlocking 5 mile trail system consists of several well marked gentle trails allowing for easy navigation, some are suitable for wheelchairs and seniors with mobility challenges. There are several access points to Oak Creek where you can swim or just cool your heels. The visitor center is a great place to pick up a little education on the local wildlife, along with learning more about Sedona. There are bathroom facilities which are always welcome.

For additional information check out their web site at https://azstateparks.com/red-rock/

Red Rock State Park Details

Dogs are not allowed in the park
Park Hours: 8 am to 5 pm * Last entry at 4:30 pm
Visitor Center: 9 am to 4:30 pm
Extended Summer Hours: Friday through Sunday

8 am to 6:30 pm * Last entry 6 pm

Visitor Center: 9 am to 6 pm

Park Entrance Fees - Adult (14+): $7.00 / Youth (7–13): $4.00 / Child (0–6): FREE

Red Rock State Park - Kisva Trail

Distance: .< 1 Mile Out and Back

Difficulty: Easy

Total Ascent: 75 feet

Estimated Time: 35 min but you may wish to take much longer

Info: Kisva is the Hopi word for Shady Water, which describes this walk along the river. A variety of birds abound in the cottonwoods by the river. See how many ones you can identify. The trails in Red Rock Park easily combine should you wish for a longer stroll.

Red Rock State Park - Eagles' Nest Trail

Distance: 1.5 Miles Loop

Difficulty: Easy - Moderate

Total Ascent: 341 feet

Estimated Time: 1 hr 15 min

Info: This trail provides a nice variety of terrain, high red flats, a nice riparian area along the river, and some uphill to get your heart pumping. You will be glad you made the climb once you catch the views from the top of Eagles Nest. Many people choose to combine it with the Kisva Trail which makes for a slightly longer hike. You will have the opportunity to observe birds, animals and a variety of high desert vegetation.

Red Rock State Park - Apache Fire

Distance: < Mile Out and Back

Difficulty: Easy

Total Ascent: 137 feet

Estimated Time: 30 min

Info: This one will pique your interest as the trail leads to the 1946 adobe style home of Jack and Helen Frye, early settlers of Sedona (the home is closed to the public). The path will take you over Oak Creek via Kingfisher Bridge along the river where you may get a chance to glimpse the resident river otters.

These trails are part of a network of interconnecting loops consisting of 5 miles in total.

7

Vortex

Many people travel to Sedona in search of spiritual enlightenment. I am so blessed that I walk in peace and communion with my Creator. I understand not everyone can make that statement. Some seeking a deeper spiritual connection believe a Vortex allows them a deeper spiritual experience. So just what is a Vortex, as you might imagine this is a subject of much controversy. Some long term Sedona residents swear the whole idea was dreamed up by a couple of real estate agents back in the 80s. Others find great connection at these sites. There appears to be no scientific justification for what some identify to be a Vortex. There is likely little scientific evidence for many beliefs which we consider spiritual. Thus I encourage you to make your own determination about the validity of the Sedona Vortex. I have friends who can feel the energy and friends who feel nothing. You will have fun finding out if you are someone who feels a Vortex or a non-feeler.

Some say all of Sedona to be a Vortex, but there are also specific places where it is said the energy is stronger. I have listed a few of the well known Vortex for your consideration. You will note that most of the ones I have listed are a subset of a hike I have already listed above. I was actually a little surprised by the overlap. I started by listing the hikes that I like best. I then dug into areas identified with strong Vortex. So maybe I am a feeler after all. In any case you will notice below I have specified the areas most often identified as the strongest energy field of the specific Vortex.

Airport Trail Vortex
   Distance: 3 Mile Loop
   Difficulty: Easy to Moderate
   Total Ascent: 415 feet
   Estimated Time: 1 hr 30min
   Directions: From the junction of Routes 89A and 179, take 89A west 1.0 miles to Airport Road on the left. Go 0.5 miles and park in the turnout on the left.
   Parking: If there are no places available at the turn out you will need to pay a fee and park at the airport, the red rock pass does not apply to this parking area.
   Info: Take the spur marked Overlook Trail to the top to find the Vortex. If you choose to do the whole trail please note the trail may not be suitable for children as there are some areas with rather steep drop offs. This Vortex is easily accessible as it is in the heart of Sedona. It is not unusual to find people meditating at this spot so please be respectful. Sunsets can be extra special here as you watch the sun go down, the city lights up and feel the evening air settle in around you. As always, take plenty of water and put on good footwear as the trail can be rocky.

Bell Rock Vortex
   Distance: 1 Mile Out and Back
   Difficulty: Easy

Total Ascent: 400 feet or more if you choose to climb higher

Estimated Time: 1 hr

Parking: Best Choice NorthernMost Bell Rock parking lot

Alternate SouthernMost Bell Rock parking lot which will add 1 mile to hike.

A Red Rock Pass (or America The Beautiful Interagency Pass, Golden Age or Golden Access) is required. You can purchase online here https://www.recreation.gov/sitepass/74387

Info: Bell Rock is one of the most iconic formations in Sedona. It is actually located in what I consider a suburb of Sedona called the Village of Oak Creek. You can't go wrong with Bell Rock as the whole area is a Vortex. Some say the best spot is at the north slope. My son will sometimes drive down from Flagstaff after work just to do this hike to relax. I like it because it is so conveniently located in The Village of Oak Creek where the vibe is just a little more laid back from the rest of Sedona.

Cathedral Rock Vortex

Distance: 1.2 Miles Out and Back

Difficulty: Hard

Total Ascent: 741 feet

Estimated Time: 1 hr 10 min

Parking: Monday through Wednesday plan on coming early to secure a parking place.

A Red Rock Pass (or America The Beautiful Interagency Pass, Golden Age or Golden Access) is required. You can purchase online here https://www.recreation.gov/sitepass/74387

Thursday through Sunday you will not be able to park here you must use the free shuttle. Click this link to obtain all the latest info https://sedonashuttle.com

Info: It will require more stamina to access this Vortex. The first half of the trail provides great places for reflection and not much physical exertion. The second half is a different matter. Please do not attempt this if you are not in good shape. You will need to make sure you are wearing hiking boots and physically prepared. This part of the trail will require hands and feet to scramble up some sections. You will find the Vortex in the saddle of the two pillars.

Boynton Canyon Vortex

Distance: 1.2 Miles Out and Back
Difficulty: Easy
Total Ascent: 500 feet
Estimated Time: 1hr 15min
Parking: Best to arrive early to get a parking space.

A Red Rock Pass (or America The Beautiful Interagency Pass, Golden Age or Golden Access) is required. You can purchase online here https://www.recreation.gov/sitepass/74387

Info: Take the Boynton Canyon Trail to the Boynton Vista Trail. This trail will lead to the Vortex at the base of the rock spires, look for the Kachina woman. This is an easy trek, great for the whole family. If you worked up an appetite check out Enchantment.

Chapel of the Holy Cross

Take Hwy 179 to Chapel Road 780 Chapel Rd, Sedona, AZ 86336
Distance: Short walk from parking lot to chapel
Difficulty: Easy
Total Ascent: apx. 50 feet
Estimated Time: 30 min
Parking: Generally there is more than enough parking

Info: The Chapel of the Holy Cross is considered to be one of the strongest Vortex in Sedona. Depending upon your faith consider lighting a candle and saying a prayer for a loved one.

Take time to read the history of the Chapel. It is inspirational.

Chapel of the Holy Cross

8

Conclusion

In conclusion

I hope that you will find Sedona is indeed a magical place.

In this quick and easy guide I have shared with you what I share with friends and family.

I provided a brief overview of how Sedona is laid out.

The activities I enjoy, a day at the spa, wine tasting, ballooning, and biking (my family enjoys this one).

I have shared a few awesome hikes along with things you need to know to enjoy the trails and stay safe.

Now all that's left to do is to go out and explore the beauty of Sedona.

Enjoy!

9

Resources

10 Best Hikes and Trails in Sedona. (2022). Alltrails.Com. Retrieved June 28, 2022, from https://www.alltrails.com/us/arizona/sedona

Coconino National Forest - Airport Loop Trails. (2022). US Forest Service. Retrieved June 29, 2022, from https://www.fs.usda.gov/recarea/coconino/recarea/?recid=71905

Coconino National Forest - Boynton Canyon Trail No. 47. (2022). US Forest Service. Retrieved June 28, 2022, from https://www.fs.usda.gov/recarea/coconino/recarea/?recid=55242

Coconino National Forest - Cathedral Rock Trail No. 170. (2022). US Forest Service. Retrieved June 29, 2022, from https://www.fs.usda.gov/recarea/coconino/recarea/?recid=55264

Coconino National Forest - Courthouse Butte Loop Trail. (2022). US Forest Service. Retrieved June 29, 2022, from https://www.fs.usda.gov/recarea/coconino/recarea/?recid=72016

Coconino National Forest - Devils Bridge Trail No. 120. (2022). US Forest Service. Retrieved June 29, 2022, from https://www.fs.usda.gov/recarea/coconino/recarea/?recid=55292

Coconino National Forest - West Fork of Oak Creek No. 108. (2022). US Forest Service. Retrieved June 28, 2022, from https://www.fs.usda.gov/

recarea/coconino/recarea/?recid=55432

J. (2022, April 13). *How to Hike the Bell Rock and Courthouse Butte Loop Trail*. Earth Trekkers. Retrieved June 26, 2022, from https://www.earthtrekkers.com/bell-rock-courthouse-butte-loop-trail-hike

Metzler, B. (2021, April 13). *What to do if you see a snake on a trail: expert tips to help keep your flesh fang-free*. Advnture.Com. Retrieved June 29, 2022, from https://www.advnture.com/features/what-to-do-if-you-see-a-snake-on-a-trail

Naylor, R. (2022). *What is a Vortex*. Visit Sedona. Retrieved June 29, 2022, from https://visitsedona.com/spiritual-wellness/what-is-a-vortex

Red Rock State Park in Arizona | USA. (2022). Red Rock State Park. Retrieved June 29, 2022, from https://azstateparks.com/red-rock

Sedona, Arizona Climate - 86336 Weather, Average Rainfall, and Temperatures. (2022). World Climate. Retrieved June 28, 2022, from http://www.worldclimate.com/climate/us/arizona/sedona

Sedona Shuttle. (2022, March 8). *Sedona Shuttle - The free, easy and eco-friendly way to explore some of Sedona's favorite trails!* Retrieved June 28, 2022, from https://sedonashuttle.com

Sedona Tourism Bureau. (2022). *Red Rock Pass Program Q & A*. Visitsedona.Com. Retrieved June 28, 2022, from https://visitsedona.com/trip-planning/red-rock-pass-program-qa

US Forest Service. (2021, December 20). *Staying Hydrated When Hiking in the Desert Southwest*. Grand Canyon Backpacking Trips |. Retrieved June 29, 2022, from https://fsguides.com/staying-hydrated-when-hiking-in-the-desert-southwest

Vukovic, D. (2021, October 25). *5 Steps for Calculating How Much Water to Bring Hiking*. Mom Goes Camping. Retrieved June 30, 2022, from https://momgoescamping.com/how-much-water-to-bring-hiking

Printed in Great Britain
by Amazon